CASTLES & FORTS

▼ The Citadelle Laferriere was constructed between 1804–1817 on t[he] Caribbean island of Haiti to protect the newly independent island from possib[le] invasions by its former colonial ruler, France. It was designed by Germ[an] engineers who were then imprisoned inside the fortress out of fear that th[ey] might reveal the secrets of its construction. The fortress is now [a] UNESCO (United Nations Educational, Scientif[ic] and Cultural Organization) Wo[rld] Heritage Si[te]

CASTLES & FORTS

Simon Adams

Foreword by

Professor Clifford J. Rogers

KINGFISHER

BOSTON

Publishing manager: Melissa Fairley
Coordinating editor: Caitlin Doyle
Senior designer: Peter Clayman
Picture manager: Cee Weston-Baker

Production controller: Debbie Otter
DTP manager: Nicky Studdart
DTP operator: Primrose Burton
Artwork archivists: Wendy Allison,

Jenny Lord
Proofreader: Sheila Clewley
Indexers: Sylvia Potter, Sheila Clewley

KINGFISHER
a Houghton Mifflin Company imprint
222 Berkeley Street
Boston, Massachusetts 02116
www.houghtonmifflinbooks.com

First published in hardcover in 2003
First published in paperback in 2007
10 9 8 7 6 5 4 3 2 1

1TR/1206/TWP/MA(MA)/130ENSOMA/F

LIBRARY OF CONGRESS CATALOGING-IN-PUBLICATION DATA
Adams, Simon, 1955–
    Castles and forts / Simon Adams.—1st ed.
        p. cm.—(Kingfisher knowledge)
    Includes index.
    Summary: An illustrated exploration of a wide array of castles and
    fortifications throughout the world, from Norman mottes to Maori forts,
    including how and why they were built and their importance in history.
        1. Fortification—Juvenile literature. 2. Castles—Juvenile literature. [1.
    Fortification. 2. Castles.] I. Title. II. Series.
UG401.A33 2003
322.7—dc21   2003044631

ISBN 978-0-7534-6119-8

Printed in Singapore

Contents

NOTE TO READERS
The Web site addresses listed in this book are correct at the
time of going to print. However, due to the ever-changing
nature of the Internet, Web site addresses and content
can change. Web sites can contain links that are unsuitable
for children. The publisher cannot be held responsible for
changes in Web site addresses or content or for information
obtained through third-party Web sites. We strongly advise
that Internet searches are supervised by an adult.

GO FURTHER . . .
INFORMATION PANEL KEY:

 Web sites and
further reading

 career paths

 places to visit

▼ The ramparts of Agadir, on the Atlantic coastline of Morocco in Africa, were built in the 1540s to protect the town's casbah (castle) and to keep an eye on the neighboring Portuguese, who had built a fortress in the town and wanted to expand their control along the coastline.

Foreword

Most of the fortresses in America were built in the 1800s and 1900s to guard our ports against threats from overseas. Most American children know the story of Fort McHenry in the War of 1812—the inspiration for the national anthem—but only a few have stood in the shadows of the fort's massive walls, and soaked up the sense of history that seems to fill the air there. Even fewer have been lucky enough to walk the weathered parapet of a one-thousand-year-old castle in England or France. Yet we all have castles in our minds. We imagine them when we read tales of King Arthur or histories of the Crusaders and see them in movies or on television. They are powerful symbols, calling to mind the history of the Middle Ages and days of war and chivalry, when many ideas and institutions of modern times first developed. They also represent more abstract ideas—like strength, timelessness, and independence. In their own time they were much more than just symbols (though they were that, too). Forts and castles were sometimes instruments of tyranny or conquest, sometimes shelters against violent raiders or determined invaders. They were homes for garrisons of soldiers and sources of great pride for noble lords and ladies. They were storehouses for grain and gunpowder and centers of administration and government. More human effort over the millennia has gone into building fortifications than into any other form of grand public architecture, including the construction of temples and cathedrals.

Castles and Forts will help you educate your imagination and your eye so that when you encounter a grim fortress in a book or on a screen—or in person—you will better understand why it looks the way it does, how it was built, how it would have been defended or attacked, and what it was like to live in one of its towers. You'll find out why medieval townspeople were willing to put forth the incredible effort it took to build dual belts of stone walls, how Japanese castles were similar to and different from European ones, and why spiral staircases in fortresses normally go up with a clockwise twist. You'll see how one thousand years of new ideas and new technology transformed the simple wooden keep on its raised motte to the elaborate, sunken defenses of Verdun. If you get to visit a Revolutionary War fortification like Fort Putnam at West Point (which was a key defensive site long before it became the home of the United States Military Academy in 1802), you'll understand some of the long, long history of architechtural design that influenced its plan. The beautiful and accurate illustrations on every page of this book will make you feel almost like you are there at Masada with the Roman legions or defending Ticonderoga against the redcoats—if you put your imagination to work and try to feel the cool, moist surface of rough-hewn stone, smell the wood-smoke and roasting meat on the cookfires, hear the dull echoes of boots marching down long hallways. Make the journey now, in your mind. Later, if you can, make it in person and see and touch and explore for yourself one of these exciting reminders of the world's warlike history.

Professor Clifford J. Rogers
West Point, New York

Iron Age stone fort at Inishmore, Ireland

CHAPTER 1

The first forts

No one knows exactly when the first fort was built—or where it was—but we do know why it was built. Our ancestors needed to defend themselves against hostile tribes and wild animals, so they built simple defenses out of wood around their houses and farms. Later the first civilizations in the Middle East and then Greece built fortified citadels, or strongholds, out of brick and stone that were both palaces and places of refuge for the local population. Most cities had walls or earthen ramparts (protective barriers made out of dirt) around them and guarded entrances that could be closed at night or during times of danger. The Chinese even built a wall around their entire country!

By the time of the Roman Empire, 2,000 years ago, large-scale fortresses were being constructed to house the Roman legions and to subdue the local people.

Bronze Age fortifications

From the middle of the 200s B.C.—when the ancient
Egyptians were building pyramids and other civilizations
and empires in the Middle East and India were constructing
palaces, temples, and fortified cities—Europeans were
defending themselves against attacks in fortified villages.

Living in fear

The people who lived in central and northern Europe
4,500 years ago were settled farmers who grew cereals,
vegetables, fruit, and crops such as flax for making linen.
They kept herds of sheep, goats, and cattle and used stone
and bronze to make tools and weapons. Their major
concern—besides producing enough food to eat—was
safety both for themselves and their livestock. Wild animals,
such as wolves, roamed the forests, while hostile tribes were
always ready to attack. In order to defend themselves
our Bronze Age ancestors fortified their villages with
walls made of wood.

Wooden walls

Most of these villages were built on the shores of lakes o
by rivers—often located on small islands that could easil
be fortified. A group of around 20 rectangular houses sto
on stilts built to cope with seasonal flooding. The houses
had walls made of timber planks and roofs made of reed
with gaps at the top to let out the smoke. Pathways mad
of split logs ran between the houses, along which roame
goats, sheep, pigs, and other animals alongside wooden
racks used to dry fish, meat, and animal hides. Running
around the outside of the entire village was a high
timber wall in which a few strong gates were set.

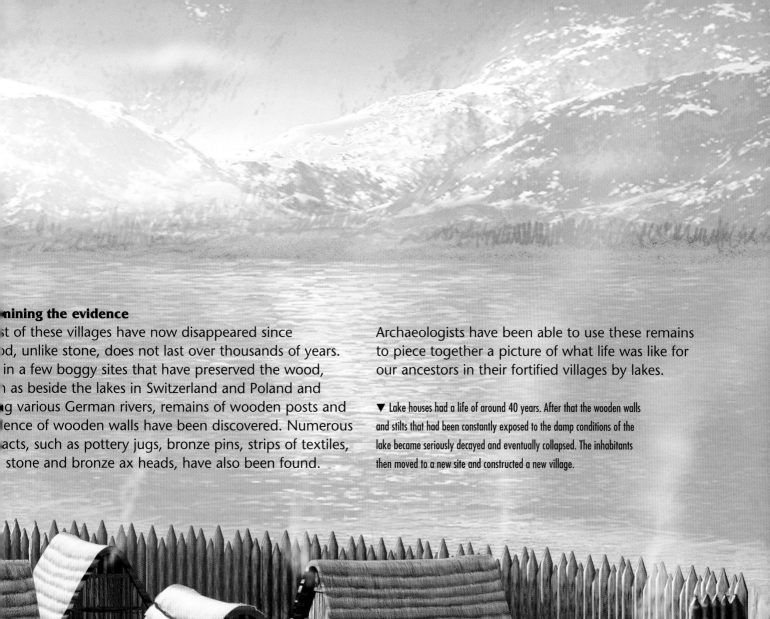

...mining the evidence

...st of these villages have now disappeared since ...od, unlike stone, does not last over thousands of years. ...in a few boggy sites that have preserved the wood, ...h as beside the lakes in Switzerland and Poland and ...g various German rivers, remains of wooden posts and ...ence of wooden walls have been discovered. Numerous ...acts, such as pottery jugs, bronze pins, strips of textiles, ...stone and bronze ax heads, have also been found.

Archaeologists have been able to use these remains to piece together a picture of what life was like for our ancestors in their fortified villages by lakes.

▼ Lake houses had a life of around 40 years. After that the wooden walls and stilts that had been constantly exposed to the damp conditions of the lake became seriously decayed and eventually collapsed. The inhabitants then moved to a new site and constructed a new village.

Maiden Castle

Think of a castle or a fort, and you immediately imagine a huge stone building towering over the countryside. But many early forts were not built out of stone but instead out of the earth on which they stood, piled up into huge ramparts several feet high. One example of this is Maiden Castle in Dorset, southern England.

What is in a name?

Do not be fooled by the name—Maiden Castle is not actually a castle but is a large hill fort. It was constructed around 300 B.C. by the ancient Britons on the site of an earlier Stone Age camp. The fort consisted of circular ramparts, each one up to 98 ft. (30m) tall, wrapped around the top of a hill two miles in circumference. The town itself covered 44 acres and contained stone and wooden houses, granaries, storehouses, the chief's house, and other buildings—all linked together by wood and gravel tracks.

▲ Vespasian (A.D. 9–79) was a very successful Roman milit commander, taking part in the invasion of England in A.D. 43 and the suppression of the Jewish revolt in A.D. 66, among o campaigns. He became the Roman emperor in A.D. 69, bring peace and prosperity to the empire until his death ten years

▶ Maiden Castle stands on top of a large hill commanding the countryside for miles around. The main entrance was guarded by a labyrinth of earthworks through which attackers would have had to find their way under a hail of slingshots before reaching the wooden gates into the town.

Roman conquest

...den Castle was both a fort and a town, a place ...re local people were protected against enemy ...es. Around 50 B.C. it became the tribal capital of the ...otriges and was one of the most prosperous towns in ...thern England. As a result, it attracted the attention of ... Romans, who invaded England in A.D. 43. A Roman ...on led by Vespasian attacked the town, massacring ...t of its inhabitants and destroying buildings. Those ... survived were taken in captivity to the nearby new ...an town of Durnovaria, present-day Dorchester.

...ch warfare

... know a lot about Maiden Castle because the ...ous British archaeologist Sir Mortimer Wheeler ...90–1977) excavated the site from 1934–1937. ...found the graves of 34 people, their skeletons ...wing the wounds inflicted by Roman swords and ...ista bolts. He also found 22,000 pebbles carried ...from the beach three miles away. The ancient ...ons used these, ineffectually, as slingshots in ...final battle against their Roman conquerors.

▲ A typical house at Maiden Castle consisted of a ring of wooden posts, possibly with a central post supporting the conical roof of timber and thatch. An entire family would live together in the house, sleeping on the floor and cooking over a wood fire. A hole in the roof allowed the smoke to escape.

The Great Wall of China

Most forts consist of a few buildings surrounded by a high outer wall. More than 2,000 years ago, however, the Chinese decided that individual forts—regardless of how many were built—could not protect their country from attacks. So they decided to turn China itself into a nation-sized fort by building a giant wall.

◄ In 221 B.C. Zheng (259–2 the leader of the northwestern state of Qin, defeated the last enemies and united all of Chin a single leader for the first tim took the title of "First Sovereig emperor," or "Qin Shi Huangdi gave his name—Qin is pronou "chin"—to the empire itself. Z only ruled until 210 B.C., but th empire he founded lasted until it was overthrown in 1912.

▲ Qin Shi Huangdi's tomb—40 mi. outside of Xi'an in central China—is guarded by 6,000 life-sized warriors and their horses and 1,400 chariots and cavalrymen—all made out of terra-cotta and armed with bronze weapons. The figures were individually modeled and arranged in rows in three underground chambers. They stood undiscovered for more than 2,000 years until they were unearthed in 1974.

hworks

Great Wall of China began around 400 B.C. as a long
es of earthen walls. It was built to mark the frontiers
ween the various Chinese states and to act as a barrier
prevent the barbarian nomads of Mongolia and
nchuria from sweeping south into the fertile plains of
thern China. Around 214 B.C. the first Chinese emperor,
Shi Huangdi, ordered these walls to be linked together
rebuilt into a continuous stone fortification that
tched 1,497 mi. (2,415km) along the entire northern
tier of his new empire. Huge groups of laborers were
fted from all over China to build this wall—many of
om died during its complicated construction.

A moving wall

Over the years the wall was strengthened and extended
west, often along new routes, until the Ming emperors,
who ruled China from 1368–1644, rebuilt the wall farther
to the south than the first structure. Their wall—the one
we see today—is more than 2,480 mi. (4,000km) long,
running from the Gulf of Liaodong in the east across the
mountains of northern China to the deserts of the Gansu
province in the west. The wall is an average of 6 ft. tall, with
a 5-ft.-wide base that slopes to a width of 4 ft. at the top.
Watchtowers along its length housed cannons and other
armaments, while the wide walkway along its top allowed
space for soldiers to move quickly in times of danger.

▼ The Great Wall of China is said to be the only man-made object that is visible from the Moon, but since it
is not much wider than an average road that is impossible! It is not unique—the Romans built a similar wall
across northern England to keep out the hostile Scots— but it is the longest man-made structure in the world.

Masada

In A.D. 66 the Jews rose up in a revolt against the Roman Empire. They fought a long and violent gue war against the occupying Roman army, which in respor inflicted large-scale destruction throughout Judea (now pa of Palestine). After the capture of the Jewish capital, Jerusale in A.D. 70 a few extremists continued to fight, making their last and dramatic stand at the hill-top fortress of Masada.

Royal stronghold

The site of the fortress of Masada consists of a flat-topped rocky outcrop, 23.5 acres in size. Masada was first fortified by the Jewish kings during the 100s B.C. Then, from 37–31 B.C., it was extensively rebuilt as a palace and personal stronghold by Herod (ruled 37–4 B.C.), king of Roman-occupied Judea at the time of the birth of Christ. Herod surrounded the flattop of Masada with high walls, and inside them he built two royal palaces, a synagogue, heated bathhouses, and storehouses.

◀ In A.D. 70 Roman troops led by Titus (A.D. 39–81, Roman emperor from A.D. 79–81) besieged and occupied Jerusalem, destroying the Jewish temple and many other buildings. The Arch of Titus in the Forum in Rome, Italy is a commemoration of this victory.

▼ The Roman army was best in the world at the t but it was no match for t Jewish guerrilla forces. T well-armed Romans pref to fight in open combat o battlefield. The Jews avoi this, instead assaulting th Roman infantry with slin and javelins and retreati the hills when attacked.

The Jewish revolt

After Herod's death in 4 B.C. Roman soldiers garrisoned Masada until they withdrew at the beginning of the Jewish revolt in A.D. 66. The Zealots, a fanatical Jewish sect, then occupied Masada, using it as a base for their guerrilla activities against the Roman forces. When the Romans finally captured Jerusalem in A.D. 70, the Zealots withdrew to a few well-defended fortresses. One by one the Romans captured these as well, until only Masada remained in Jewish hands.

The Roman siege

In A.D. 72 the Roman commander Flavius Silva (Roman governor of Judea from A.D. 71–81) began the siege of Masada, encircling the garrison so that none of its occupants could escape. He then constructed an earthen ramp up to the western side, on top of which he built a stone siege tower, and moved up battering rams and catapults. By the spring of A.D. 73 Silva was ready to attack.

▲ Archaeologists discovered the pottery lots at Masada in 1963. They found that one belonged to Ben Ya'ir. It is possible that he was the last man alive and that he killed himself after killing the remaining men.

[...] t of what we know about the final stand at Masada [...] from Flavius Josephus (born A.D. 37), a Jewish priest [...] vernor of Galilee who supported the rebels until he was [...] d by the Romans in A.D. 67. He then changed sides, [...] ng a Roman citizen and writing histories of the Jews.

[...] s suicide

[...] de Masada the leader of the Zealots, Ben Ya'ir (died [...] 73), made a drastic decision. He ordered the entire [...] ess, except the food supplies, to be burned to show that [...] were acting out of pride, not desperation. Ya'ir then [...] red the married men to slay their own families before [...] wing straws to select ten of them to kill the rest of the [...] ison. The ten then drew straws again to select one of [...] n to kill the other nine before killing himself. When the [...] omans broke in, they were met not by an army as they expected but by a graveyard. Masada has remained a symbol of Jewish resistance ever since.

▼ Masada stands on a rocky outcrop overlooking the Dead Sea and the Judean desert in the southeast of what is now Israel. Its water supply came from huge underground cisterns and aqueducts cut into the solid rock, while most of its food was grown on the flat, fertile ground on the top of the outcrop.

Castel Sant'Angelo

Most castles undergo a few changes in their use during their lives, possibly evolving from a fortified strongho into a military headquarters and then a private residence. But none has undergone such a dramatic transformation as the Castel Sant'Angelo—the Castle of the Holy Angel—i Rome, Italy, which began life not as a castle but as a tomb

▲ Successive popes from 1390 onward turned the castle into a luxurious papal palace, commissioning the most famous artists and sculptors of the day to decorate the many papal private apartments, chapels, and staterooms. Pope Clement VII (in office from A.D. 1523–1534) hired Giovanni da Udine (1487–1535) to paint the elaborate frescoes in this bathroom.

The imperial tomb

In A.D. 123 the Roman emperor Hadrian (ruled A.D.117–138) decided to build an impressive mausoleum (tomb) next to the banks of the Tiber river in Rome. He designed the building himself based on an earlier magnificent tomb built for Emperor Augustus (ruled 27 B.C.–A.D. 14) one century earlier. The mausoleum consisted of a square plinth (base) 283 ft. (86.3m) long. Set on top of this was a cylindrical structure 210 ft. in diameter and covered on top with earth and planted with cypress trees. A small, round building sat on the top. Hadrian's tomb and rooms for future burials were in the center of the mausoleum, linked by a long gallery to an entrance on the riverbank. Ivory-colored marble covered the entire structure, which was decorated with numerous statues.

◄ Roman soldiers successfully protected the mausoleum from attacks until the Roman Empire fell in A.D. 476. However, in A.D. 537 an Ostrogoth army from northern Italy besieged it. Roman defenders broke up Castel Sant'Angelo's many marble statues and used their heads, arms, and legs as ammunition to hurl down on top of their attackers.

almost one century the mausoleum entombed the
erial bodies, but by A.D. 275 it had become part of the
sive walls built to protect Rome from attacks. By A.D. 500
as used as a prison.

On August 29, 590 Pope Gregory I (in office from 590–
) led a procession through Rome asking God to rid the
of the plague. When they approached the mausoleum,
skies darkened, and a rainbowlike figure of an archangel
eared overhead. The plague lifted, and from then on the
usoleum became known as the Castle of the Holy Angel.

al palace

ing the next 1,000 years the castle played an
ortant part in the turbulent history of Rome, serving
h as a fortress and as a place of refuge for successive
es. In 1277 a fortified walkway was built from the
can to allow popes quick access to the castle in times
anger. After it was severely damaged by an uprising in
7 Pope Boniface IX (in office from 1389–1404) began
k in 1390 to turn the castle into a papal palace. In
0 the castle was used as a barracks
military prison before becoming the
seum it is today.

▲ In 1527 the mercenary army of the Holy Roman Emperor Charles V
(ruled 1519–1556) mutinied against their commanders. They sacked Rome
in an attempt to make themselves rich, looting its beautiful buildings and
killing at least 30,000 people. Pope Clement VII fled to Castel Sant'Angelo,
where he was besieged for six months before reaching an agreement
with Charles V.

ring the 1600s the bridge connecting the
leum to the other bank of the Tiber river
ecorated with ten statues of angels by the
s sculptor Gian Lorenzo Bernini (1598–1680),
it the name Ponte Sant'Angelo (Holy
s Bridge).

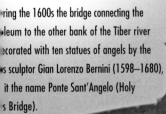

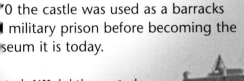

Ait Benhaddou

The ksar (fortified village) of Ait Benhaddou might look familiar to you—even if you have never been to eastern Morocco, in Africa. But look closely at movies such as *Lawrence of Arabia*, and you will see the village and its surrounding landscape on the screen—this stark but beautiful land has featured in several Hollywood movies.

▲ The Berbers are skilled craftspeople, producing beautiful handicrafts. Even their swords and scabbards are ornate, made of beaten silver and inlaid with other metals and precious gems.

People on the move

Morocco has had a complex history, with successive waves of Phoenician, Carthaginian, Roman, Vandal, Arab, Saharan, Spanish, and French traders and conquerors stamping their marks on the country. As a result, the Berbers and other Moroccan tribes were pushed into the remote mountainous regions. Many of them fortified their villages to protect themselves against these and other hostile forces.

Safe trade

Ait Benhaddou stands on the historic trade route from the Moroccan city of Marrakech south across the Sahara desert to the great trading post of Tombouctou (Timbuktu). It was built by the Berbers, although no one is sure about the exact date, and it has since been added to many times. Like every ksar, it is protected by an impressive set of walls and towers.

gical colors

merchants of Ait Benhaddou grew wealthy from trade,
ding many impressive casbahs (castles) to protect themselves.
other villagers lived in small houses crowded together on the
ide, using the igherm (communal granary) to store their grain.
these buildings were made of sun-baked bricks of earth mixed
water and straw. Due to its history and beauty Ait Benhaddou
ow one of UNESCO's (United Nations Educational, Scientific,
Cultural Organization) World Heritage Sites.

Berbers and other Moroccans are renowned for their
riding skills. Displays of horsemanship, known as
sias," are performed according to strict rules.
ders gallop very fast, holding their
p in the air. At a signal from
der they all fire
son.

▶ Most Moroccan
medinas (towns), such as
Taroudant (right), are
enclosed by high walls,
with numerous look-out
towers along their length.
Gates into the medina
are heavily fortified.

SUMMARY OF CHAPTER 1: THE FIRST FORTS

Fort or castle?

You will already have realized that the difference between a fort and a castle (and a fortress and a fortification) is not very clear. Maiden Castle might sound like it should have had stone walls and battlements—just like a medieval castle—but it was, in fact, a large hill fort made out of earth; while the fortress of Masada had high walls around it and was used as a residence, just like a castle.

In reality the words are often interchangeable. A castle is technically a large fortified building or set of buildings, while a fort is a fortified enclosure with buildings inside of it. A fortification (or fort for short!) is a defensive structure such as an earthwork, wall, or tower, and a fortress is a large fort. But do not be confused since all of these definitions imply a military structure of one type or another—even if their owners or keepers are not very clear when it comes to deciding whether they want their structures to be known as castles or forts.

Rillaton gold cup c. 2000 B.C.
(early Bronze Age artifact)

Where in the world?

The forts and castles in this chapter range from fortified lake settlements in northern Europe to converted mausoleums in Rome and *ksars* or fortified villages in Morocco. We could have visited many other ancient forts and castles in almost every continent in the world—with the exception of Australasia, where the aborigines had no need to build permanent structur at this time.

What all of these castles and forts have in common i that they were built by people who had a need to defer themselves and their livestock against attacks. All of ther take advantage of natural features, such as hilltops or lake and many of them also command major trading routes dominate important cities. It takes walls and ramparts t create a fort or castle, but most importantly it also requi a good location to make sure that it is as secure as possib

Go further . . .

Dig out more information about archaeology:
www.digonsite.com

Explore Maiden Castle and other English Heritage sites:
www.english-heritage.org.uk

Learn more about the Great Wall of China:
enchantedlearning.com/subjects/greatwall

For more information on Masada:
http://mosaic.lk.net/g-masada.html

Awesome Archaeology by Nick Arnold (Scholastic, 2001)

Eyewitness Archaeology by Jane McIntosh (Dorling Kindersley, 1998)

Archaeologist
Studies the remains of ancient forts.

Conservationist
Preserves ancient remains.

Tour guide
Escorts visitors around historic sites.

Computer graphic artist
Recreates ancient sites on screen.

Illustrator or **photographer**
Documents the ancient sites.

Historian
Writes about ancient forts and castles.

Surveyor
Maps ancient sites.

Visit Maiden Castle (c. 300 B.C.), an ancient British hill fort.
www.english-heritage.org.u

Explore Fort Sumter—in person and the National Park Service Web site fo information on visiting, photos, links and a brief history of the fort.
Fort Sumter
Sullivan's Island, SC 29482
Phone: (843) 883-3123
www.nps.gov/fosu

Explore Fort Ticonderoga—in person and on their official site for a list of eve visitor information, and photo gallery.
Fort Ticonderoga
Ticonderoga, NY 12883
Phone: (518) 585-2821
www.fort-ticonderoga.org

CHAPTER 2

The great age of castles

tarting in the A.D. 800s local rulers began building castles to defend themselves and their families from attacks by their enemies. These castles were first made of wood and then were replaced later with much more complex structures constructed of stone and brick. Towering above the countryside, castles were often the biggest and most impressive buildings in the area.

They served as homes and fortresses, headquarters and prisons, and incorporated the latest thinking in building design, construction, engineering, and military technology. For more than 800 years these castles and their owners dominated the political, military, and geographical landscape—not just in Europe but as far afield as India, Japan, the Middle East, and South America.

Alcazar de Segovia, Spain

Motte and bailey castle

In Western Europe the first castles appeared in the A.D. 800s and 900s, a time of great lawlessness. Local lords built simple wooden ringworks (enclosures) on top of earthen ramparts that were surrounded by ditches—in order to protect themselves and their families from invaders. These simple structures began a period of castle building that lasted for almost 800 years.

▲ The first castles to be built in Western Europe consisted of a simple fortified bailey with a bridge leading up to a protected motte, or mound. Quick and easy to build, these castles were very effective at defending their occupants.

▼ The Bayeux Tapestry (below) records the building in Hastings, southern England, of a motte about one week before the great battle on October 14, 1066 when William of Normandy won the English crown. The workers were probably local Saxons who were forced into service by the Norman army. A finished motte castle (right) is shown later in the tapestry.

The Norman invasion

The first castles were built to protect their inhabitants from attacks, as well as to provide a safe garrison (military post) for local soldiers. But by the 1000s A.D. castles were mainly used as bases to help subdue the local peasants. The reason for this great change was the 1066 conquest of England by William of Normandy, France. Faced with a hostile Saxon population, King William needed to assert his authority over his new kingdom.

The motte and bailey

William brought with him a design for a castle he had developed in Normandy. This consisted of a wooden-fenced bailey (courtyard) surrounded by a moat and protected by a dirt rampart. Within the bailey were stables, workshops, a well, and possibly even a chapel. Separated from the bailey by its own moat was the motte—a mound of pressed layers of soil at least 16 ft. high—on which a wooden tower and a lookout post stood. The only access to the motte was by using the drawbridge.

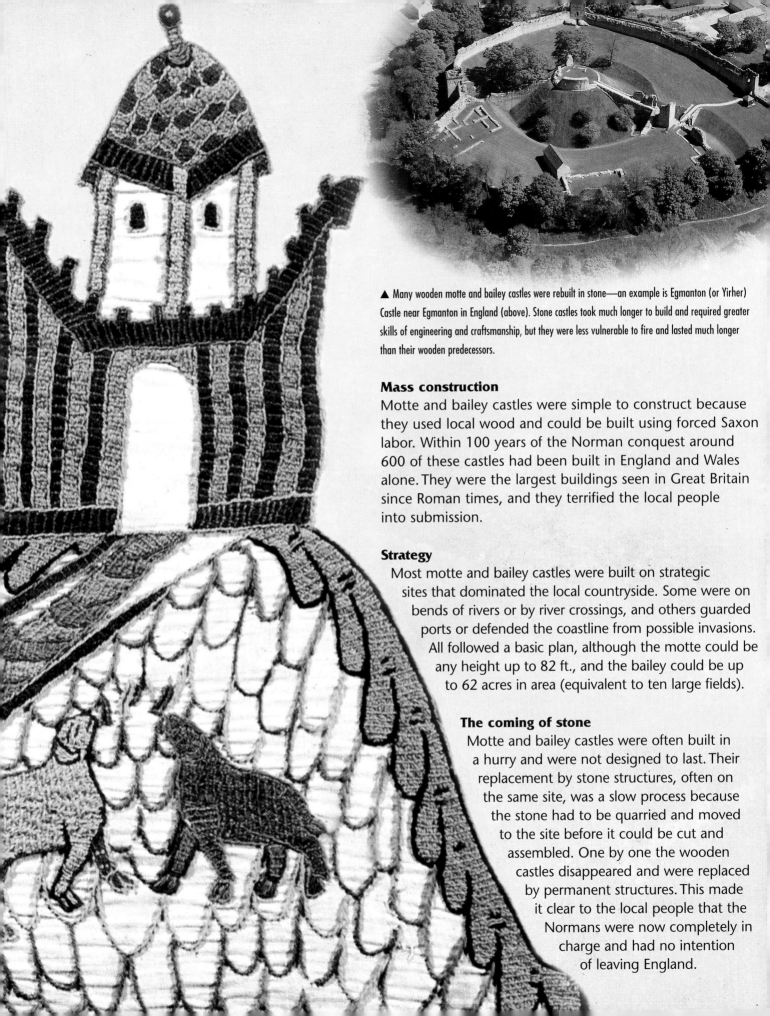

▲ Many wooden motte and bailey castles were rebuilt in stone—an example is Egmanton (or Yirher) Castle near Egmanton in England (above). Stone castles took much longer to build and required greater skills of engineering and craftsmanship, but they were less vulnerable to fire and lasted much longer than their wooden predecessors.

Mass construction

Motte and bailey castles were simple to construct because they used local wood and could be built using forced Saxon labor. Within 100 years of the Norman conquest around 600 of these castles had been built in England and Wales alone. They were the largest buildings seen in Great Britain since Roman times, and they terrified the local people into submission.

Strategy

Most motte and bailey castles were built on strategic sites that dominated the local countryside. Some were on bends of rivers or by river crossings, and others guarded ports or defended the coastline from possible invasions. All followed a basic plan, although the motte could be any height up to 82 ft., and the bailey could be up to 62 acres in area (equivalent to ten large fields).

The coming of stone

Motte and bailey castles were often built in a hurry and were not designed to last. Their replacement by stone structures, often on the same site, was a slow process because the stone had to be quarried and moved to the site before it could be cut and assembled. One by one the wooden castles disappeared and were replaced by permanent structures. This made it clear to the local people that the Normans were now completely in charge and had no intention of leaving England.

Building in stone

The first stone castles appeared in western Europe during the A.D. 900s. Over the next 600 years these giant structures dominated the countryside, acting as the headquarters of the local lord, a garrison for his army, a house for his family, and a prison for his opponents.

The appearance of stone

The first stone castles were constructed in the late A.D. 900s either at Langeais or Doué-la-Fontaine in western France—historians are unsure which one came first. Many more were built after the Norman Conquest of England in 1066 as permanent stone structures replaced the wooden motte and bailey castles (see pages 22–23) quickly erected after the invasion. Among these were Chepstow (c. 1067) on the border of England and Wales, the Tower of London (work began on the stone White Tower in 1078), and the huge Rochester Castle (c. late 1060s) guarding the strategic Medway river crossing on the road between the English Channel and London.

▶ Castle windows were not designed for allowing light in and especially not for looking at the view! Technically known as arrow loops, or arrow slits, their only function was to allow an archer to fire his arrow or crossbow at the enemy without being hit by the return fire. The only windows with glass would have been in the chapel.

▶ Spiral staircases revolved in both directions, but most went up clockwise (like this one at Rochester Castle), allowing a defending soldier to fight with his sword in his right hand while retreating up the steps. Some spiral staircases went up from the ground floor straight to the roof, with a hidden staircase giving access to the floors in between. These staircases—and other defensive devices—were designed to confuse an intruder.

The great tower

At first stone castles consisted of a single large donjon (tower), often known as a keep. These towers could be any shape—square, rectangular, or round—and had giant stone walls, narrow slits for windows, and a single entrance, often raised up above the ground and approached by an exterior staircase. The tower contained both living quarters for the lord and his family and lodgings for his soldiers. Later curtain walls were built around the tower, creating a large bailey where animals could be kept and horses stabled. Fortified gatehouses, often including a portcullis, protected the entrance, while a drawbridge over the moat provided extra defense for the people inside the walls.

Slow work

Each castle was built to its own design and varied from place to place according to the wealth and needs of its owner and the quality of the local stone. Building was a slow process—on average, a tower rose ten feet (3m) per year. As the stone was quarried an army of laborers transported it to the site, which had already been cleared. Skilled masons then cut and placed the stone. Once built many castles were whitewashed—the White Tower of London gets its name from the whitewash applied to it during the A.D. 1200s—while others were coated in plaster. The cost of construction was high— historians estimate that up to ten percent of the English national budget from 1155–1215 was spent on castle building.

Château Gaillard

The impressive fortress of Château Gaillard stands on a loop of land sticking out into the Seine river in northern France. It was constructed between 1195 and 1198 by one of the most famous kings in medieval Europe, Richard I, king of England, and was supposed to be impregnable. However, by 1204 it had fallen to the troops of his fiercest enemy, Philip II of France.

England in France

As king of England, Richard I (ruled 1189–1199) had inherited huge estates in northern and western France. But most of Richard's French possessions were also claimed by the French kings, who resented the huge power the English had in France. Richard I decided to build Château Gaillard to protect his frontier from French invasions.

▲ Richard I was king for ten years, but he only spent seven month[s] [in] England. The rest of the time he fought in crusades in the Holy Lan[d] [(]pages 28–29) or tried to protect his French empire from Philip II. He [was] renowned for his bravery and nicknamed "Coeur de Lion"—the Lion[.]

▼ At the center of Château Gaillard was the great keep with walls more than 8.2 ft. thick. The fortress had three courtyards and was protected by three huge stone walls, each one up to 29.5 ft. high. A giant moat surrounded the outer walls.

Belfry—a movable siege tower made of wood

Traction trebuchet to hurl rocks and other missiles

...Is made of butter!

...English king built his castle on a rocky ridge ...ft. above the Seine river to dominate the surrounding ...ntryside. He boasted he could hold his castle "even if ...walls were made of butter." But he died before his claim ...ld be put to the test, and his brother John became king.

...siege

...ip II first attacked Château Gaillard in 1203, ...n encircling the castle itself. The English commander, ...er de Lacy, drove out all the women, children, and ...rly from the castle in order to save his food supplies ...the soldiers. But Philip II refused to accept them, ...ing them all to spend the winter shivering and ...gry near the castle moat until he eventually relented. ...In the spring of 1204 the siege began in force. The ...ch hauled up catapults and a belfry and began filling ...castle moat so that they could approach the outer ...ls on level ground. Protected by mantlets—large ...den shields—sappers (miners) began to undermine ...of the outer towers. According to one contemporary ...rce, the tower came tumbling down.

▲ After the siege Château Gaillard was repaired by its new owners until, in 1603, Henry IV (ruled 1589–1610) ordered that its defensive walls should be dismantled. Over the years the stone was taken away and used in the construction of many local buildings, leaving the castle in the ruined state we see today.

Victory

The French rushed into the outer courtyard and discovered an unguarded latrine shaft, which gave them easy—if smelly —access up through the walls to the middle courtyard. There they drew up a trebuchet and began to attack the thinner, innermost walls. Sappers begain working, and these walls came tumbling down, too. As the French stormed in the English garrison surrendered, and the 140 defenders were taken prisoner. Château Gaillard was now in French hands.

Spring-loaded catapult to hurl
flaming missiles and rocks

Concentric castles

During the second half of the A.D. 1200s a new type of castle appeared in Western Europe, many of them built by Edward I of England. The concentric castle—with a double ring of defensive walls and other groundbreaking features such as a reinforced gatehouse—was based on an old design, but it proved incredibly effective in keeping out attackers.

▲ Edward I, who ruled England from 1272–1307, was nicknamed "Hammer of the Scots" after his attempt to unite the kingdoms of England and Scotland.

The need for change

The first stone castles had been constructed with a single outer wall. This was strong and tall but was vulnerable to siege engines and mining works. Once the wall was undermined or fell down the siege was effectively over, and the castle was easily occupied. A better system of defense was needed to make a castle truly impregnable.

▼ The first concentric castle built in Great Britain, Caerphilly Castle was constructed between 1268–1271 by Gilbert de Clare (1243–1295)—the most powerful English baron in south Wales— during his campaign against the Welsh prince Llywelyn ap Gruffydd (ruled 1246–1282).

[In]spiration from the East

[The] solution to this problem came from
[an u]nlikely source—the ancient walls
[of C]onstantinople in Turkey, built
[by E]mperor Theodosius II between
[AD] 410–447. In order to protect
[the] eastern capital of the Roman
[Emp]ire, Theodosius encircled the
[city] with two sets of walls only
[60 ft.] apart. The inner walls were
[arou]nd 29 ft. tall; the outer were
[15 ft.] tall. Both walls had huge
[prot]ruding towers along their length
[at re]gular distances. In front of these
[wall]s was a deep moat, only bridged
[at t]he five main entrances to the city.
[From] the time of their construction
[to t]he arrival of the crusaders in 1204
[the] walls had never been breached.

[W]inning design

[It w]as the crusaders who brought this new design back
[to W]estern Europe. This design was used to build their
[own] castles, including Krak des Chevaliers (see pages
[30–]31) in the biblical Holy Land (what is now Israel
[and] Palestine). The concentric design was incredibly
[effec]tive since defenders on the high inner walls could
[fire] over the heads of their fellow defenders on the
[lowe]r outer walls without (usually) harming them.
[If] required, the defenders on the outer walls
[coul]d also rush out to attack the besieging enemy,
[conf]ident that the castle remained well defended
[from] its inner walls. Cylindrical towers stood at each
[corn]er of the inner walls, while access to the castle was
[limit]ed to one or two heavily fortified twin-towered
[gate]houses. The overall design varied from site to site,
[and] many of these new castles were regular in shape,
[and] some were almost perfectly square.

◀ Concentric castles
were not only built in Great
Britain. Muiderslot in the
Netherlands—*slot* means
"castle" in Dutch—was built
around 1280 and clearly
shows the influence of King
Edward's Welsh castles.

▲ Edward I spent much of his reign in battle—first against the Welsh and then the Scots. New
castles were built to subdue the Welsh, while existing ones were fought over for control of Scotland.

Concentric castles soon appeared across Europe.
Existing castles were given new outer sets of walls,
while ten new castles were built by Edward I in north
Wales to subdue the area after its conquest in 1282. This
tremendous work of castle building involved 150 masons
and 400 carpenters, as well as 1,000 diggers and 8,000
woodcutters to clear the land before construction began.
Many towns, such as Carcassonne (see pages 36–37) in
France, were also fortified by concentric walls.

▼ This aerial view of Caerphilly castle in Wales demonstrates its concentric design, strong gatehouses,
and surrounding moat. These features made it the strongest castle in south Wales.

Krak des Chevaliers

In 1095 Pope Urban II (in office from 1088–1099), head of the Christian church in Western Europe, issued a call to arms. The Muslim Seljuk Turks, who controlled the biblical Holy Land (what is now Israel and Palestine), were preventing pilgrims from traveling from Europe to holy sites such as Jerusalem. The pope promised spiritual benefits to those who would fight to reclaim the land from the Muslims. Thousands of crusaders from many countries answered his call and traveled to the Holy Land. There they built a series of castles, including Krak des Chevaliers.

Copying the enemy

Krak des Chevaliers, in modern-day western Syria, was a Muslim fortress until it was captured in 1099 by the crusaders. In 1144 the crusader ruler of the area gave the fortress to the Knights Hospitallers, a religious order of knights who turned it into the vast and impressive castle we see today.

Krak des Chevaliers—the Castle of Knights—stands above the west bank of the Orontes river, from where it could command the strategic north-to-south route from Syria to the Holy Land. The castle could only be approached from one direction, making it almost impregnable. But the Knights Hospitallers took no chances when rebuilding Krak des Chevaliers. They copied many of the Muslim fortifications they had encountered on crusade.

▼ The Crusades lasted from 1095 to 1291, when the final Christian stronghold in the region, Acre, fell to the Muslims. Thousands of knights from all over Europe sailed to the Holy Land or took the more dangerous overland route through Turkey. Despite this huge endeavor, the crusaders failed to remove the Muslims from the Holy Land.

▲ During the final siege in 1270 siege engines caused great damage to the outer walls and towers. Catapults hurled huge missiles against stonework to weaken the structure, while trebuchets launched burning balls of tar and straw to set fire to interior woodwork.

Building for strength

The basic plan of the castle was concentric (see pages 28–29), but the Hospitallers added many extra features. The inner wall consisted of huge, interconnected towers overlooking a moat, which served as a reservoir to supply water to the knights. The outer wall, added in the early 1200s, included several semicircular towers that could deflect any missiles fired at them by siege engines.

A crucial weakness

Despite its huge strength, Krak des Chevaliers had one major weakness. All the water in the castle flowed into it from the surrounding hills along an aqueduct. If the aqueduct was blocked, the castle would run out of water—a serious problem in such a hot region.

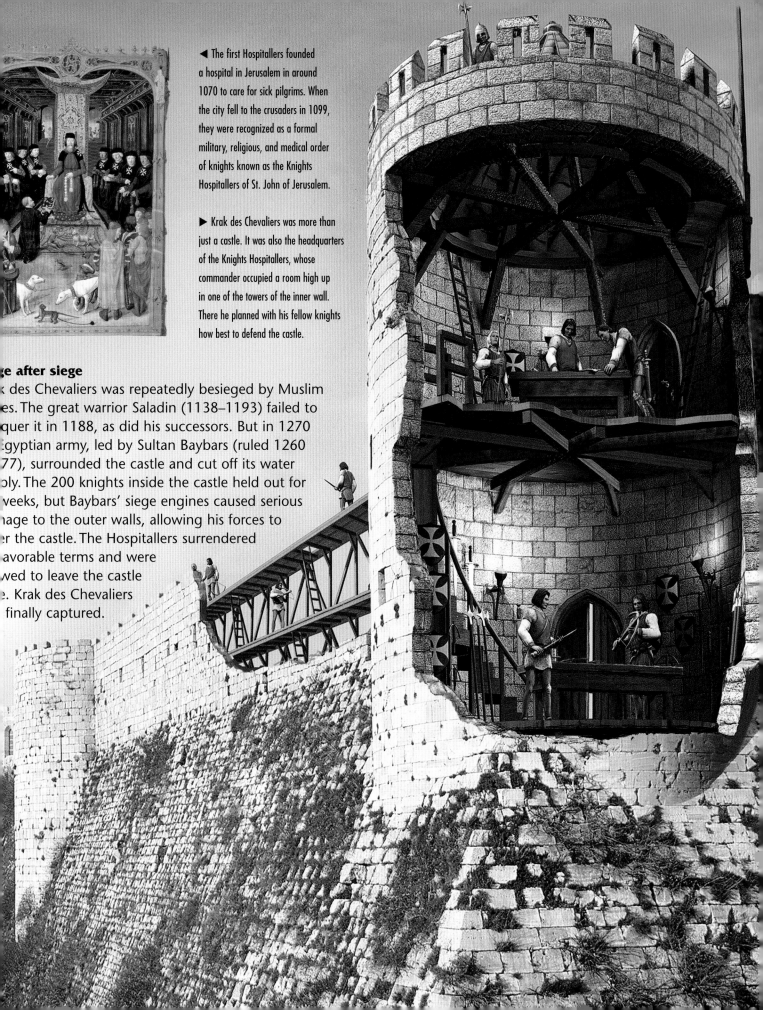

◀ The first Hospitallers founded a hospital in Jerusalem in around 1070 to care for sick pilgrims. When the city fell to the crusaders in 1099, they were recognized as a formal military, religious, and medical order of knights known as the Knights Hospitallers of St. John of Jerusalem.

▶ Krak des Chevaliers was more than just a castle. It was also the headquarters of the Knights Hospitallers, whose commander occupied a room high up in one of the towers of the inner wall. There he planned with his fellow knights how best to defend the castle.

...e after siege

...k des Chevaliers was repeatedly besieged by Muslim ...es. The great warrior Saladin (1138–1193) failed to ...quer it in 1188, as did his successors. But in 1270 ...gyptian army, led by Sultan Baybars (ruled 1260 ...77), surrounded the castle and cut off its water ...ply. The 200 knights inside the castle held out for ...weeks, but Baybars' siege engines caused serious ...mage to the outer walls, allowing his forces to ...er the castle. The Hospitallers surrendered ...avorable terms and were ...wed to leave the castle ...e. Krak des Chevaliers ...finally captured.

Riverbank castles

Sail on the Rhine river today, especially the stretch between Mainz and Cologne (Köln) in Germany, and you are immediately struck by the large number of castles on both riverbanks. But only a few of these impressive buildings began as castles, most having the much less exciting role of collecting tolls (taxes) from passing ships.

▲ In Poland stone replaced wood as the main building material for castles much later than in the rest of Western Europe because wood was the most easily available building material. The original wooden Bedzin Castle (above), in Poland, was destroyed twice by fire before Casimir the Great (ruled 1333–1370) finally rebuilt it in stone.

Robber barons

In the Middle Ages the Rhine was not the peaceful river it is today. Rival German kings and princes fought for control of the river and its lucrative trade. They built castles along the banks to control the flow of people and goods and exacted high tolls that they used to enrich themselves and their families. Some of these princes were known as robber barons because their tolls were so high.

The robber barons acquired such incredible power that the main trading cities on the river—which were badly affected by the high tolls they had to pay to ship goods from one city to another—formed the League of Rhenish Cities in 1254 to challenge them. In 1272 the German emperor, Rudolf I (Holy Roman emperor from 1273–1291), came to the cities' aid and crushed the barons for good. Four of their castles were captured, others were weakened, and gradually peace was restored.

The toll tower

However, local rulers still needed to collect tolls. One such ruler was Louis the Bavarian (Holy Roman emperor from 1314–346), whose family held extensive lands in the Rhine valley. In 1327 Louis built a five-sided tower—the Pfalzgrafenstein—on a small islet in the Rhine, from which his ships could row or sail out onto the river and intercept any passing craft. They collected any tolls due and made sure the river was not being used for any hostile purposes.

▲ Louis the Bavarian, here seen in a more saintly manner, built Pfalzgrafenstein to collect river taxes and to assert his control over a stretch of the Rhine river.

► Standing on a rocky islet off the east bank of the Rhine, Pfalzgrafenstein is the only Rhineland castle actually built on the river.

► The castle commander's room is situated in the tower, from where he could watch the river and its traffic. Although the interior has changed over time, the room clearly shows that this was an administrative building, not a fortified military installation.

The "Ship of Stone"

In 1337 the Pfalzgrafenstein tower was surrounded by a six-sided building with high walls on the outside that protected the domestic buildings inside, creating a typical German-style turret fortress. The castle soon became known as the "Ship of Stone" because it appeared to sail majestically on the river itself. Over time the castle has undergone many modifications. But while it was occasionally used for war, its main purpose has always been to collect money from river users.

The Alhambra of Granada

Think of a castle or fortress, and you probably picture a forbidding building with huge, stone walls, almost n decoration, and very little comfort or luxury. In most cases this is true, but in southern Spain there is a remarkable fortress that is more like a villa with beautiful gardens.

A beautiful fort

The Alhambra of Granada was built between 1238–1358 by the Moors—Muslim Arabs from northwest Africa who invaded and conquered most of Spain in A.D. 711. The Moors were skilled fighters who needed a secure fortress from which to control their southern Spanish kingdom, but they were also a very cultured people who valued fine architecture, beautiful design, and luxurious living.

▼ Inside the Alhambra are n formal gardens, complete with water and lush greenery. The de la Acequia forms part of th Generalife, or summer palace, in the grounds of the main palace.

t for protection

name Alhambra comes from the Arabic word
"red," the color of the sun-dried bricks of the outer
s. The fortress stands on top of a hill, and its outer
s, with their 23 towers and four gateways, were built
defense. Inside, however, the buildings served several
erent purposes. There were mosques for worship, seven
ces for the Moorish princes to live in, a fortress for the
iers, a prison, and even a royal mint. These were set
ng lush, water-filled gardens and were connected to
other by covered walkways—all designed to keep
palace cool and shady in the hot summer months.

agic palace

pite its beauty, the Alhambra was also a violent place.
ornate Hall of Abencerrajes got its name after one of
Moorish princes beheaded all of the *abencerrajes* (sons
is first wife) so that his son by his second wife could
eed him. The Moors were expelled from their palace
492 when the Catholic rulers of Spain, Ferdinand and
ella—joint leaders who united the country by their
riage—finally drove them out of Spain. The Moors'
cy is one of the most beautiful buildings in the world.

▲ Water is carried to the Alhambra along a 1-mi.-long covered
watercourse from the hills nearby. Once inside the building
it supplies the numerous fountains, pools, basins, and water
channels that decorate the interior and its many courtyards.

▶ The rows of stone columns and arched windows of the
Alhambra are all intricately decorated with geometric patterns.
The decoration is made of plaster that was applied to the stone
and then engraved while it was still wet. Elsewhere mosaic tiles
add even more decoration to the floors and lower walls.

◄ This aerial view of Carcassonne gives a clear idea of the scale and complexity of its fortifications. Sitting on top of a hill, its concentric walls, heavily fortified citadel, and giant barbican (seen in the center foreground) made the city almost impregnable.

The great walled fortress towns of Europe

Ever since the first large towns and cities were built around 6,000 years ago in the Middle East, urban inhabitants have always protected themselves with defensive walls. These defenses developed into state-of-the-art fortifications during the Middle Ages—especially in Western Europe.

The need for walls

Europe during the Middle Ages was a much more lawless place than it is today. Real power often rested in the hands of the king's feudal lords, who held great lands of their own and commanded private armies. Rivalry between these lords often broke out into warfare, which meant towns had to protect themselves in case they were attacked by enemy forces. A strong wall around a town or city could keep its inhabitants safe at night.

New defenses

Many towns used existing Roman fortifications, adding to or strengthening them as required. As a further safeguard a fortified citadel was often built into the walls to house the garrison and the town's administration, while a second set of walls was built around the first set to provide a double line of defense. Towers were built at even distances along the walls—both as lookouts and as platforms from which arrows and missiles could be fired down. Entrance to the town was controlled through a highly secure barbican (gatehouse) fortification.

▲ Carcassonne is surrounded by a set of concentric walls—with 17 towers on the lower, outer wall and 29 towers on the higher, inner wall.

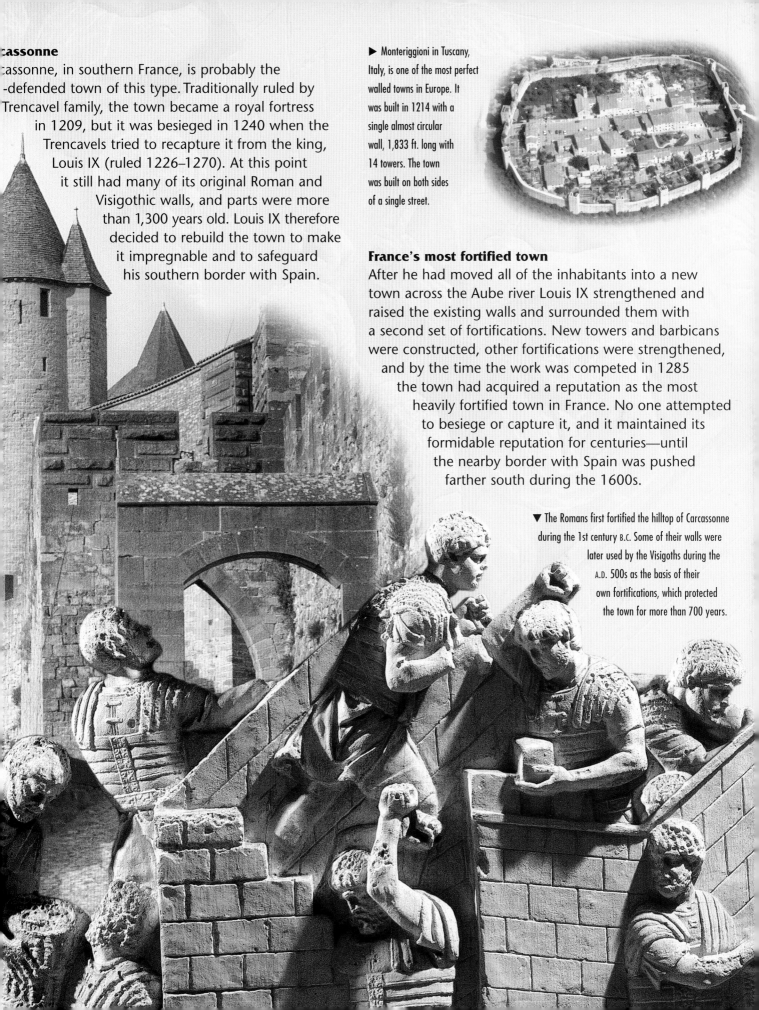

Carcassonne

Carcassonne, in southern France, is probably the best-defended town of this type. Traditionally ruled by the Trencavel family, the town became a royal fortress in 1209, but it was besieged in 1240 when the Trencavels tried to recapture it from the king, Louis IX (ruled 1226–1270). At this point it still had many of its original Roman and Visigothic walls, and parts were more than 1,300 years old. Louis IX therefore decided to rebuild the town to make it impregnable and to safeguard his southern border with Spain.

► Monteriggioni in Tuscany, Italy, is one of the most perfect walled towns in Europe. It was built in 1214 with a single almost circular wall, 1,833 ft. long with 14 towers. The town was built on both sides of a single street.

France's most fortified town

After he had moved all of the inhabitants into a new town across the Aube river Louis IX strengthened and raised the existing walls and surrounded them with a second set of fortifications. New towers and barbicans were constructed, other fortifications were strengthened, and by the time the work was competed in 1285 the town had acquired a reputation as the most heavily fortified town in France. No one attempted to besiege or capture it, and it maintained its formidable reputation for centuries—until the nearby border with Spain was pushed farther south during the 1600s.

▼ The Romans first fortified the hilltop of Carcassonne during the 1st century B.C. Some of their walls were later used by the Visigoths during the A.D. 500s as the basis of their own fortifications, which protected the town for more than 700 years.

Himeji Castle

Towering above the Harima plain of central Japan, the imposing wooden fortress of Himeji was built to withstand every bullet or arrow an enemy could fire at i But ironically it never saw a shot fired in anger, and it sc became a palatial residence for the local daimyo (lord).

▲ The Japanese samurai was a trained warrior who fought for his daimyo and was served by local peasants. The daimyo and their samurai held great local power in Japan until a strong central government took control in the early 1600s.

The first castle

During the Middle Ages Japan was a largely lawless country with rival daimyo fighting each other for power and influence. In 1580 one such daimyo, Hashiba Hideyoshi (1536–1598), decided to build a castle in Himeji in order to strengthen his control over the local area. At first the castle only consisted of a simple three-storied fortified tower, called a *tenshukaku*, but by 1609 the new daimyo, Ikeda Terumasa (1564–1613), had added several other buildings and fortifications to it, creating today's magnificent structure.

▲ The outer corridors of Himeji stored muskets and lances ready for use. The double rows of pegs were used as gun racks, while fire beaters hung on the hooks near the ceiling.

Fortifying the castle

Himeji Castle is surrounded by a moat, and one channel tucks in behind the other in order to form a double barrier. Lining the inside of the moat are high walls and fortified gatehouses, protecting the outer courtyards. A series of raised fortifications and additional gatehouses protect the network of inner courtyards. At the heart of this complex stands the main eight-storied keep of Himeji, linked by lower buildings to three smaller keeps. The building's wooden frame rests on stone so that it will "bounce" if there is an earthquake, a common occurrence in Japan.

▶ Himeji Castle has been nicknamed "White Heron Castle" because its curved roofs and white, plastered walls reminded people of the bird often seen in Japan.

main keep

main keep was designed to be impregnable.
tands on a raised plinth (base) of rock and dirt and
oated with fireproof, bulletproof white plaster to protect
wooden framework. To enter this fortress invaders had
ush through a series of fortified entrances and twisting,
row passages. Inside the keep the defenders were well
pared. Hidden openings under the roofs allowed them
drop rocks, hot oil, and boiling water onto the enemy.
The gunports were tilted downward
to get the best angle of fire.

▲ The Japanese believed that the larger and more elaborate the roof and gables
were, the greater the power and prestige of the owner of the building. At Himeji
the roofs of the castle have a wealth of decoration and detail, with highly
decorated gables, giant overhangs, and ornate wooden shingle tiles.

Out-of-date

Himeji Castle was built at a time when small firearms,
such as handguns and muskets, were first introduced
into Japan. Cannons were rare, which
meant a well-designed, well-defended
castle, such as Himeji, could have
withstood almost any siege. However,
the castle was built just as the period
of political instability in Japan
was coming to an end. In
the early 1600s the great
shogun (warlord) Ieyasu
Tokugawa (1524–1616) broke the
control of the powerful daimyo and
their samurai supporters
and introduced a
period of prolonged
peace to the country.
Himeji was then unnecessary
and became a luxurious
residence instead.

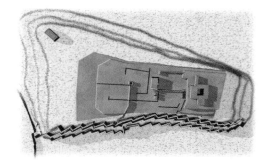

▲ The Incan capital Cuzco (or Cusco) was built in a rigid grid pattern, with the fortress of Sacsahuaman to its west (top left of this plan).

Sacsahuaman

When the Spanish conqueror Francisco Pizarro arrived in the Incan empire in South America in 1532, he hoped to find gold and silver. He did find those in abundance, but what he also discovered was one of the most awe-inspiring buildings in the entire world—the stone-built fortress of Sacsahuaman.

The Incas

The Incan empire expansion began in the 1430s and soon stretched along 1,984 mi. (3,200km) of the Pacific coast of South America, from modern-day Ecuador in the north down through Peru and Bolivia to Chile in the south. The Incas created one of the most technologically advanced civilizations in the world. They built a huge road network, constructed suspension bridges to cross over the many river gorges in their mountainous empire, and terraced and irrigated the steep hillsides for agriculture. Most important of all, they built fabulous cities and palaces, protecting them with impressive fortresses such as Sacsahuaman.

▼ The Incas never discovered the wheel, so they had to drag the locally quarried stones to the site using rollers and manual labor. They then used pulleys and ramps to raise them up into position. Each stone was individually cut and shaped so it fit exactly into place.

Impressive stones

Sacsahuaman—an Incan word meaning "satisfied falcon"— was built in the mid-1400s to defend Cuzco, the Incan capital. The fortress was more than 1,738 ft. long and consisted of three huge terraced walls, in some places rising to more than 66 ft. and built in a zigzag design to deter attacking forces. Inside these walls were three massive towers—the largest of which had a 69-ft.-long rectangular base and rose up five stories. The fortress easily housed 5,000 soldiers. In times of crisis the entire population of Cuzco could retreat inside its walls.

The Incas were masterful stonemasons. To build Sacsahuaman they first created a small-scale model in clay. They then cut, finished, and individually shaped each stone using bronze and stone chisels and hammers and sandpaper. The Incas were so skilled that each stone fit exactly into place so that not even a thin blade could be inserted alongside it. Some of the stones at Sacsahuaman are huge—the largest still at the site is 4,061 ft.^{3} (115m^3) and weighs more than 360 tons.

end of an empire

...pite its size and strength, the Incan empire was no
...ch for the Spanish. In May 1532 Pizarro and his small
...y of 240 men and 62 horses invaded the empire. They
...k advantage of a civil war to quickly capture and kill the
...an emperor, Atahuallpa (died 1533). Pizarro seized Cuzco in
...vember 1533, but the Incas retreated inside Sacsahuaman.
...ee years later, after a bloody battle, the Spanish broke the
...e and finally captured Sacsahuaman. Over the next 20
...rs they deliberately dismantled the fortress
...hat, by 1560, little of it survived.

▶ Francisco Pizarro
(1475–1541) was
a Spanish explorer
who led expeditions
along the Pacific coast
of South America.
In 1532 he and his
small army invaded
and conquered the
vast Incan empire.

Golconda

Stand in the domed entrance to Golconda Fort and clap your hands, and the noise you make can be clearly heard at the highest point in the fort—almost one half mile away! This is no accident of acoustics but instead an ingenious security system designed to alert the rulers of the fort that an unwelcome guest was at their gates. The rest of this Indian fort is just as extraordinary.

▲ The fabulous Koh-i-noor—mountain of light—diamond was mined near Golconda in the early A.D. 1300s. After a long and colorful history that took it to northern India, Iran, and Afghanistan it has finished up in one of the British royal crowns. Once an incredible 1,000 karats in weight, it has been recut many times to its current weight of 108.9 karats (0.77 oz.). Legend says that only a woman can wear it because it will always bring disaster to a man.

▼ Golconda consisted of a walled city inside of which were numerous palaces, mosques, government buildings, shops, and houses. Dominating the city from its granite hill was Golconda Fort. Other palaces and forts stood outside of the city walls.

The shepherd's fort

Golconda lies on a hill to the west of the central Indian city of Hyderabad. Legend says that in the A.D. 1200s a shepherd boy came across an idol on the hill, which he took to the local king. The king constructed a clay-brick fort on the site, which became known as "Golla Konda"—meaning shepherd's hill in the local Telugu language. In 1512 Golconda became an independent state. During the next 62 years its new Muslim rulers—the Qutub Shahi kings—rebuilt the fort out of stone, as well as constructed a new city alongside it. New palaces, mosques, and many other buildings were built—all designed to let in a flow of cooling breeze during the hot summer months. Water was piped into every building and throughout the landscaped gardens that contained many fountains and bathing pools. The entire fort and city complex was surrounded by heavily fortified outer walls around seven miles (11km) long.

▶ The main fort of Golconda is built on a granite hill 394 ft. Although now mostly in ruins, enough remains of the fort to show how impressive it once was. Its granite walls stretched for three and had massive ramparts and other fortifications to defend it attacks. Specially designed parapets supported long-range cannons capable of firing at a distance of 1.5 mi. Surrounding the fort was a giant city wall, which could be entered through eight gates, protected by pointed spikes to prevent warring elephants from breaking them down!

Incredible wealth

Golconda's importance came from from the diamonds and other gems mined to its southeast and then brought into the city for cutting, polishing, and setting. At the height of its glory, during the A.D. 1500S AND 1600S, Golconda became famous for its great wealth—at one time, the 6-mi.-long road from Golconda to Hyderabad was a huge street market selling diamonds, pearls, gemstones, and jewelry to traders from all over India.

So much wealth and power attracted the attention of the Mogul emperors, who had invaded India from Afghanistan in 1526 and set up a powerful and well-administered empire that soon covered all of northern and central India. During the 1680s Emperor 'Alamgir, also known as Aurangzeb, (ruled 1658–1707) led his armies south and invaded Golconda. He captured the city, but the fort held out until 1687, when 'Alamgir managed to trick his way in. After its capture it gradually fell into ruin, its glorious past fading into history.

687 Golconda finally fell to the Mogul emperor 'Alamgir, in a line of clever rulers. His successors struggled to keep e empire together, but their wealth remained huge— be seen in the fabulous robes and jewels worn by kbar Shah II (ruled 1806–1837).

SUMMARY OF CHAPTER 2: THE GREAT AGE OF CASTLES

Defense

Castles were not just built to accommodate the local lord, his family, and knights but also to keep out those whom the lord wished to be protected against. They were defensive buildings designed to keep intruders out, with every part of their design and construction directed to this purpose. The walls were high, with few outer windows, and the foundations were deep and thick, preventing the enemy from undermining the walls and causing them to fall down. Often castles were surrounded by a moat, putting an area of water between the castle and the enemy forces. Many castles had high interior walls enclosing inner courtyards—the enemy might gain access to the outer courtyard, but further offensive operations would be needed in order to seize the lord inside the main keep.

Motte castle from the Bayeux Tapestry

Attack

The construction of concentric castles in Europe in the late A.D. 1200s marked a new development in castle design. No longer were they solely defensive buildings since now the two roughly parallel sets of walls—the outer one lower than the inner one—enabled defenders on the inner wall to protect the castle, while those on the outer wall could rush out and fight the enemy beyond the castle grounds. Further changes of design meant that the entrance to the castle became increasingly elaborate, with the simple single gateway replaced by a heavily fortified gatehouse. All of these changes were designed to make the castle impregnable and its enemy vulnerable if they tried to attack.

At first soldiers attacking or defending a castle used muscle power to fire their bows and crossbows, but the introduction of gunpowder, cannons, and firearms during the A.D. 1300s gradually transformed castle design. Existing arrow slits in walls were altered to allow for handguns, while gun ports were cut into the outer walls to allow cannonballs to shoot out toward enemy lines. The role of the castle was about to change.

Go further . . .

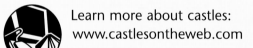

Learn more about castles:
www.castlesontheweb.com

Take a trip to the many different castles around the world:
www.castles.org

Find out more about Welsh castles:
www.castlewales.com/home.html

Castles of Britain and Ireland
by Plantagenet Somerset Fry
(David & Charles, 1996)

Eyewitness Castle by Christopher Gravett (Dorling Kindersley, 2000)

Why Are Castles Castle-Shaped?
by Philip Ardagh
(Faber Children's Books, 2002)

Stonemason
Repairs and replaces old stones.

Conservation officer
Cares for old castles.

Medieval historian
Studies the period when the great castles were built.

Armorer
Restores and repairs medieval weaponry.

Computer programmer
Creates interactive games based on castles, knights, and battles.

Web site designer
Creates web sites dedicated to castles.

Visit the Tower of London—a 1078 stone tower, fortress, royal residence, and prison.
Tower of London
London, England EC3N 4AB
Phone: 44 20 7709 0765
www.hrp.org.uk/webcode/home.a

Explore Caerphilly Castle (1268–1271) in Wales, the first concentric castle in Great Britain.
www.castlewales.com/caerphil.htm

Discover Himeji Castle in Japan, the 16th-century castle that became a palatial residence. For photos and additional resources visit:
www.greatbuildings.com/building Himeji_Castle.html

A ruined castle near the town of Kilgarvin, Ireland

CHAPTER 3

The end of an era

y the 1600s the great age of castles had come to an end. Strong central vernments throughout Europe and an guaranteed peace at home—and luced the power and ability of local ds to wage war against each other. stles were therefore no longer needed protect the local people from attacks. However, European nations still needed tresses to protect their colonial and ding interests abroad, especially in the

Americas. In the late 1800s and early 1900s A.D. a new generation of partially underground fortresses—such as France's Fort Douaumont, designed to withstand the heaviest artillery attack—was developed in Europe to defend national borders from enemy attacks.

A few romantics built their own castles in an attempt to recreate a distant time, but by the start of this century castles and forts belonged only in history.

Fort Ticonderoga

Not every fort or castle makes an impact on history. Many survive in relative obscurity, rarely participating in events of national or international importance. One exception, however, is Fort Ticonderoga, an A.D. 18th-century American fort on the narrow strip of land between Lakes Champlain and George in upstate New York. This fort made history twice and was attacked six times, all in the course of 20 tumultuous years.

▶ Fort Ticonderoga was built with wooden walls, filled with dried mud, and then covered with stone quarried from a nearby valley. Inside the fort were several buildings—including a barracks capable of holding up to 400 men and a large arsenal. The star-shaped design of the fort left no blind spots where an attacker could hide, making it difficult to attack.

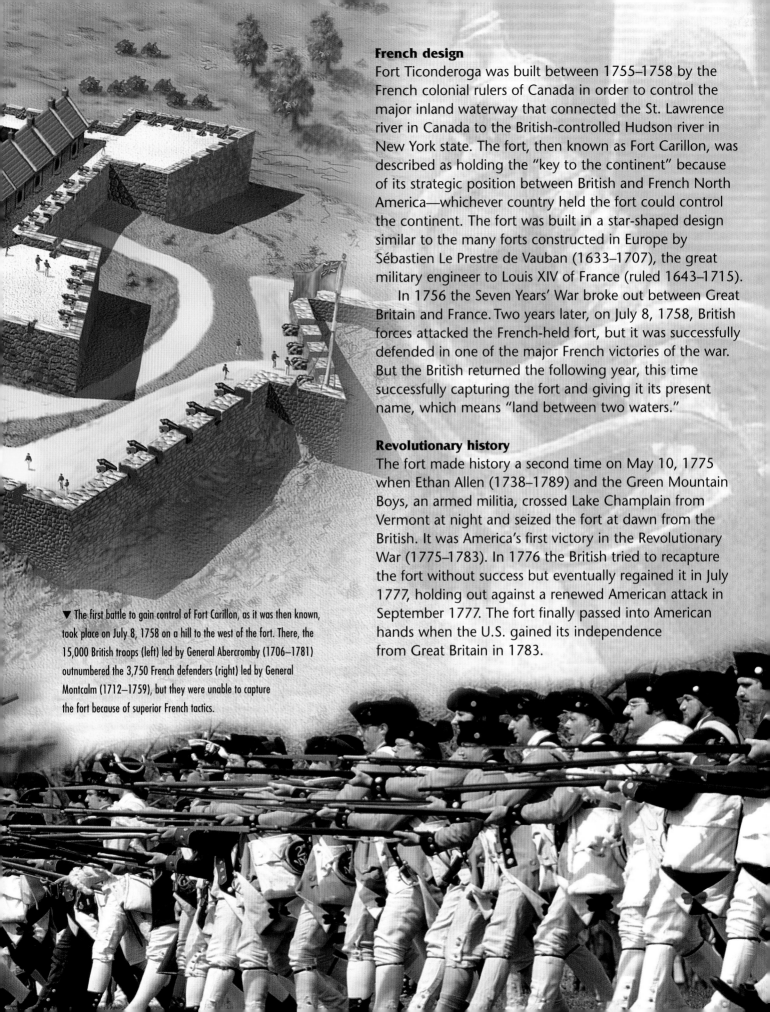

French design

Fort Ticonderoga was built between 1755–1758 by the French colonial rulers of Canada in order to control the major inland waterway that connected the St. Lawrence river in Canada to the British-controlled Hudson river in New York state. The fort, then known as Fort Carillon, was described as holding the "key to the continent" because of its strategic position between British and French North America—whichever country held the fort could control the continent. The fort was built in a star-shaped design similar to the many forts constructed in Europe by Sébastien Le Prestre de Vauban (1633–1707), the great military engineer to Louis XIV of France (ruled 1643–1715).

In 1756 the Seven Years' War broke out between Great Britain and France. Two years later, on July 8, 1758, British forces attacked the French-held fort, but it was successfully defended in one of the major French victories of the war. But the British returned the following year, this time successfully capturing the fort and giving it its present name, which means "land between two waters."

Revolutionary history

The fort made history a second time on May 10, 1775 when Ethan Allen (1738–1789) and the Green Mountain Boys, an armed militia, crossed Lake Champlain from Vermont at night and seized the fort at dawn from the British. It was America's first victory in the Revolutionary War (1775–1783). In 1776 the British tried to recapture the fort without success but eventually regained it in July 1777, holding out against a renewed American attack in September 1777. The fort finally passed into American hands when the U.S. gained its independence from Great Britain in 1783.

▼ The first battle to gain control of Fort Carillon, as it was then known, took place on July 8, 1758 on a hill to the west of the fort. There, the 15,000 British troops (left) led by General Abercromby (1706–1781) outnumbered the 3,750 French defenders (right) led by General Montcalm (1712–1759), but they were unable to capture the fort because of superior French tactics.

Fort Sumter

At 4:30 A.M. on April 11, 1861 a canno[n] shot rang out across Charleston Harbo[r] in the southern state of South Carolina. Its target was Fort Sumter. The fort itself was insignificant, but that single shot started the four-year Civil War that was to cost 600,000 lives.

The divided nation

Ever since the United States had declared its independence from Great Britain in 1776, the nation had been divided between the proslavery southern states, which needed slaves to work on their cotton and other plantations, and t[he] antislavery northern states, which objected to slavery on mo[ral] grounds. The argument between the two sides came to a head in November 1860 with the election of an antislavery president, Abraham Lincoln (president from 1861–1865). The following month South Carolina left the Union in prote[st,] quickly followed by ten more states. Together the 11 rebel states formed the new Confederate States of America.

▲ The defenders of Fort Sumter had 48 cannons, but their supply of munitions was low. As a result, they were easily outgunned by Confederate cannons from Fort Moultrie, Castle Pinckney, and surrounding artillery units on the shore.

...ing the fort

...he U.S. headed for war Confederate troops began
...eize Union military arsenals and forts. In response
...or Robert Anderson (1805–1871), commander of
... troops in Charleston, occupied Fort Sumter—a brick
...fication on a small island in the middle of the harbor.
...Confederate forces surrounded the harbor with heavy
...nons and prevented ships from bringing more men
... supplies to the fort. Anderson, 85 soldiers, and 43
...rers were besieged.

...fatal shot

...en Anderson refused to surrender, the
...federate general, Pierre Gustave Toutant
...uregard (1818–1893), gave the order to open
... The two sides battled until, at 2:30 P.M. on April 12,
...erson surrendered when Confederate shells set the
...de of the fort on fire. The Union stars-and-stripes
... was lowered, and after a formal surrender ceremony
...erson and his men were put on ships bound for
...w York, where they were received as heroes.
...response of President Lincoln to the surrender
...immediate—on April 15 he called for 75,000
...nteers to put the "insurrection" down. The
...l War had begun—a vicious, divisive conflict
... was to last until 1865.

▲ Fort Sumter was built between 1829–1830 on a sandbank at the entrance of Charleston
Harbor. It was named after General Thomas Sumter (1734–1832), a hero of the Revolutionary War
(1775–1783). In recognition of its role in the Civil War the fort became a national monument in 1948.

▼ Despite the heavy and lengthy cannon fire exchanged by both sides, no one was killed or
seriously injured in the 34-hour bombardment. At one point the Union flag was blown off of its
flagpole by a Confederate shell. Risking his life, a Union sergeant climbed the flagpole to nail
it back into place. The sergeant survived unscathed, although the flag was ripped to shreds.

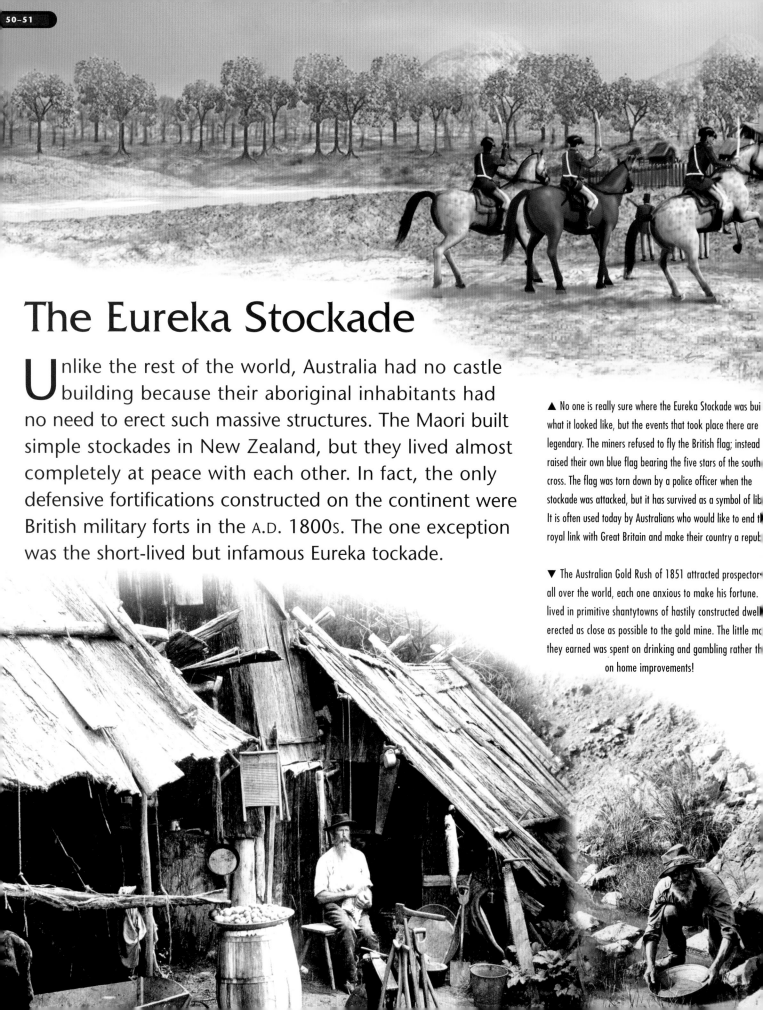

The Eureka Stockade

U nlike the rest of the world, Australia had no castle building because their aboriginal inhabitants had no need to erect such massive structures. The Maori built simple stockades in New Zealand, but they lived almost completely at peace with each other. In fact, the only defensive fortifications constructed on the continent were British military forts in the A.D. 1800s. The one exception was the short-lived but infamous Eureka tockade.

▲ No one is really sure where the Eureka Stockade was bui what it looked like, but the events that took place there are legendary. The miners refused to fly the British flag; instead raised their own blue flag bearing the five stars of the south cross. The flag was torn down by a police officer when the stockade was attacked, but it has survived as a symbol of lib It is often used today by Australians who would like to end t royal link with Great Britain and make their country a repub

▼ The Australian Gold Rush of 1851 attracted prospector all over the world, each one anxious to make his fortune. lived in primitive shantytowns of hastily constructed dwel erected as close as possible to the gold mine. The little mc they earned was spent on drinking and gambling rather th on home improvements!

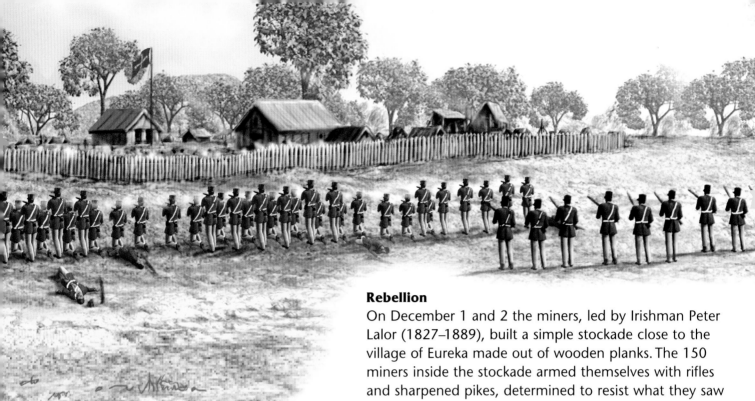

Rebellion

On December 1 and 2 the miners, led by Irishman Peter Lalor (1827–1889), built a simple stockade close to the village of Eureka made out of wooden planks. The 150 miners inside the stockade armed themselves with rifles and sharpened pikes, determined to resist what they saw as the corrupt authority of the state. Early in the morning of Sunday, December 3 troops surrounded the stockade. The miners opened fire, but they were no match for the troops, who killed 24 of them and injured another 20. The miners' rebellion was over within 15 minutes, but the Eureka Stockade has entered history as a symbol of workers' resistance to unjust authority.

Gold Rush

February 12, 1851 Edward Hargraves (1816–1891), veteran of the 1848 Californian Gold Rush, discovered in the hills around 100 mi. (160km) west of Sydney New South Wales, Australia. Further discoveries led to biggest field of all—at Ballarat, 74 mi. (120km) west Melbourne in neighboring Victoria. Prospectors rushed make their fortune—many of them were immigrants ng famine in Ireland and poverty in Great Britain. Few any respect for British authority in Australia.

wdown

British authorities tried to control the rush by ng licenses to prospect for gold, but corrupt ials abused the system, and relations with the ers deteriorated. On the night of October 6, 4 two miners tried to get a drink in the Eureka el in Ballarat, but the owner refused to let them d a fight broke out, with the owner kicking miner to death. A court acquitted the owner, e miners held a huge protest meeting. When ps were called in to keep order, the scene set for a showdown between the two sides.

Maori of New Zealand constructed wooden stockades to protect themselves enemy tribes. These simple stockades were stakes of local wood driven ground and then fastened together with ropes made of twisted vines.

Fort Douaumont

World War I broke out in Europe in 1914. Millions of people were killed and injured, many along the Western Front between Germany on one side and Great Britain, France, and their allies on the other. One of the main battles on this front took place in 1916 around the eastern French town of Verdun. The battle was bloody, but one part of it in particular was almost ridiculous.

The importance of Verdun

Verdun lay close to the border with Germany and guarded the main route to the French capital, Paris. Because of its importance, the French had surrounded the city with a series of heavily defended fortifications, including Fort Douaumont. The German army attacked Verdun and its forts in the hope that France would "bleed to death" and leave the war—but France was determined to resist.

▼ The French army used a large number of heavy artillery pieces, such as this mortar, to repel the German attack on Verdun and its many forts.

▲ Ramparts, ditches, and rolls of barbed wire surrounded the entire fort.

▲ Douaumont, like all of the forts around Verdun, was mostly underground. Originally built out of stone with a covering layer of earth, the fort was later upgraded with an 8 ft. layer of concrete placed directly above the stonework and a new 13 ft. layer of earth placed on top of that.

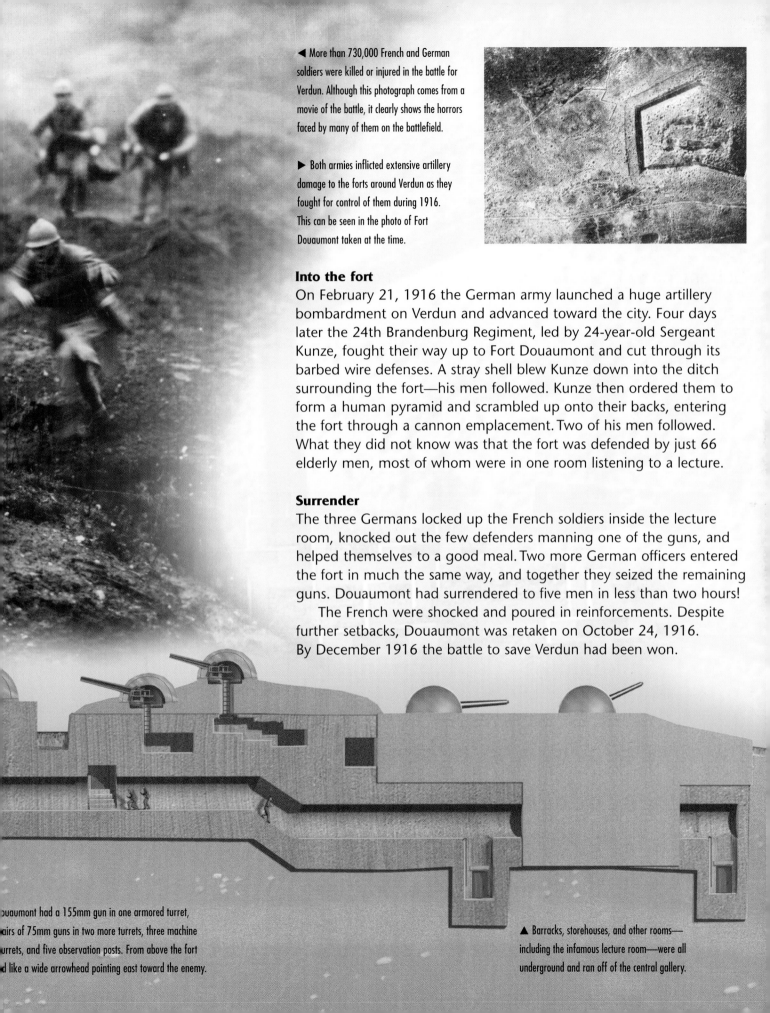

◄ More than 730,000 French and German soldiers were killed or injured in the battle for Verdun. Although this photograph comes from a movie of the battle, it clearly shows the horrors faced by many of them on the battlefield.

▶ Both armies inflicted extensive artillery damage to the forts around Verdun as they fought for control of them during 1916. This can be seen in the photo of Fort Douaumont taken at the time.

Into the fort

On February 21, 1916 the German army launched a huge artillery bombardment on Verdun and advanced toward the city. Four days later the 24th Brandenburg Regiment, led by 24-year-old Sergeant Kunze, fought their way up to Fort Douaumont and cut through its barbed wire defenses. A stray shell blew Kunze down into the ditch surrounding the fort—his men followed. Kunze then ordered them to form a human pyramid and scrambled up onto their backs, entering the fort through a cannon emplacement. Two of his men followed. What they did not know was that the fort was defended by just 66 elderly men, most of whom were in one room listening to a lecture.

Surrender

The three Germans locked up the French soldiers inside the lecture room, knocked out the few defenders manning one of the guns, and helped themselves to a good meal. Two more German officers entered the fort in much the same way, and together they seized the remaining guns. Douaumont had surrendered to five men in less than two hours!

The French were shocked and poured in reinforcements. Despite further setbacks, Douaumont was retaken on October 24, 1916. By December 1916 the battle to save Verdun had been won.

◦uaumont had a 155mm gun in one armored turret, ⸱airs of 75mm guns in two more turrets, three machine ⸱rrets, and five observation posts. From above the fort ⸱ like a wide arrowhead pointing east toward the enemy.

▲ Barracks, storehouses, and other rooms— including the infamous lecture room—were all underground and ran off of the central gallery.

Romantic castles

By the A.D. 1800s castles belonged to history. They had no military purpose—other than as army barracks or prisons—and many were falling into ruin, with their stones plundered to use in other buildings. But one man had a passion for castles, which he indulged to extravagant excess. His name was King Ludwig II of Bavaria, a small kingdom in southern Germany. His monument is the fabulous Neuschwanstein Castle, which was built not for war but for show.

▲ Ludwig II was the king of Bavaria from 1864–1886. He spent most of his money sponsoring the arts and building mock medieval castles and other follies. After he was declared mentally unfit to rule Ludwig drowned in a lake close to Neuschwanstein.

era-obsessed

...wig II had little interest in ruling his country. Instead he devoted his life ...rt and music—in particular to the operas of Richard Wagner (1813–1883), ...composer of the epic Ring Cycle of four linked operas and other works, ...om he supported lavishly. Ludwig lived in a fantasy world—he eventually ...nt insane—and dreamed of a castle inspired by Wagner's operas and their ...thical, medieval settings. He designed his private rooms in Neuschwanstein ...tle based entirely on Wagner's *Tristan und Isolde*, while the Singers' Hall ...s decorated with characters from *Parsifal*, one of the Ring operas.

...ne setting

...uschwanstein Castle was not designed by an architect but instead by a German ...ne painter who was more accustomed to working on opera sets. It took 17 years and ...uge amount of money to build, but although it looks like a medieval castle—complete ...h turrets, parapets, and battlements—it had no military function and in reality is a ...hly decorated modern home, with central heating and hot and cold running water. ...dwig died before his castle was finished—some parts are still incomplete today— ...most of it was constructed by 1892, six years after Ludwig's death.

▼ Neuschwanstein Castle sits dramatically on top of a rocky crag overlooking the peaks, valleys, and lakes of the Bavarian Alps. Its dramatic setting makes the castle look taller and more imposing than it actually is.

▲ Ludwig was not the only man to indulge his passion for castles. During the A.D. 1800s many eccentric Europeans built their own medieval castles, temples, mock ruins, and other follies such as Broadway Tower (above) in England.

Understanding ruins

As we have seen throughout this book forts and castles come in all shapes and sizes. Some have single towers, while others have large complexes of walls, courtyards, gatehouses, and moats. Some were once built of wood and others of brick and stone. Today these castles are in various stages of repair, from perfectly preserved, well-equipped working and lived-in buildings to picturesque ruins. Visit a castle today, and you could be looking at a pile of stones or asked in for dinner!

Piecing together the ruins

It is easy to see how a castle operated if the building is still in good condition, but even ruins can tell us a great deal about the life of a castle and its inhabitants. Huge foundations and thick, solid lower walls show the possible height of the main tower, while scattered stretches of ramparts and battlements can reveal something about how the castle was once defended against attacks. Even a single ruined wall can suggest the ground plan of a building or the location of a long-forgotten barbican.

Into the drains

Historians can read contemporary records, such as official state documents and personal letters, to learn about the history of a castle, but it is archaeologists who reveal the most about the life of the building itself. Using detailed scientific analysis of everything from the mortar between the stones to the smelly remains in the drains, they are able to figure out how the castle was built, where its stones came from, what its inhabitants ate, and even if they kept goats in the courtyard! They can tell us what happened to the masonry when the castle fell into ruin because local people often used the castle's stones to build their own houses and other buildings.

Chance survival

So why are some castles ruined and others are not? The simple answer is pure chance. Many castles, such as the Tower of London in England, survived by changing roles—starting as a castle and then expanding into a massive fortress and royal palace, serving as both a prison for enemies of the state and a stronghold for the crown jewels. Others, such as Maiden Castle in Dorset, England, survived for as long as their inhabitants did and were then destroyed by their conquerors. Château Gaillard survived capture by the French king in 1204 but was then dismantled by another French ruler in 1603.

e location of windows
replace in a ruined wall
how many stories the castle
ally had and where its rooms
—even if the wooden interior
collapsed long ago.

▼ This might look like a series of low stone walls, but archaeologists can examine these walls—and any pottery, bone, metal, or other fragments they uncover around them—to piece together a picture of what the building looked like and what it was originally used for.

◄ Not much remains of Dunluce Castle on the rocky cliffs of County Antrim in Ireland, but from the ruins it is possible to imagine the rectangular great hall, the circular corner towers, and the location of the drawbridge, linking it to the mainland. Your imagination will have to fill in the rest.

The castle today

Today castles and forts have many different roles. Some are still used for military purposes—as barracks or regimental headquarters rather than for defensive functions—few would stand up to an attack by modern-day artillery. Others have become prisons or storehouses. Many are private houses or, like Windsor Castle in England, royal palaces. Most, however, are in public ownership, which means that they are open to the public to visit. You can wander around the grounds, explore the keep, clamber over the battlements and even get locked in the dungeon!

Bringing the past to life

Walk through an empty castle, and it can be difficult to visualize what life must have been like so many years ago. Many castles have therefore tried to recreate their past by filling their rooms with contemporary furniture and stocking their arsenals with crossbows, rifles, and cannons. Others have full-scale museums dedicated to the castle and its role in history and publish illustrated guidebooks describing what happened where and when.

Guides take groups of people on tours of castles, explaini what a pile of old stones in the corner used to be part o or how many prisoners were drowned in the well.

Living the past

Best of all, some castles stage reenactments of historica events such as battles, sieges, and tournaments. Despite all the modern equipment, such as loudspeakers and ho dog stands, it is still possible to imagine that you are bacl in the past watching an enemy army storm the castle o that the lord and his knights are staging a tournament, complete with jousts and other events, in order to improve their battle skills and impress their womenfolk. With colorful coats of arms, shiny armor, and thunderin horses—and with fanfare blaring from the sidelines—thi is history brought to life as never before. Just for one da you can be a French knight, or a Norman soldier, or an English archer fighting for your lord and your life.

▼ It might look like a scene from the Middle Ages, but these reenactments of historical events take place in many castles today. The knights try to dress themselves and their horses just like thei medieval predecessors did, giving 21st-century tourists a good idea of what a tournament or joust might have felt like for those who took part in them hundreds of years ago.

y castles declined

st people think that castles declined in importance ause gunpowder and firearms made them easy to ick and capture. But gunpowder first appeared in ope during the A.D. 1300s, and new castles were still being built 200 years later. The real reason for their loss of importance was that society became more peaceful and stable. This meant that people could live safely in undefended country houses and stately homes without fear of attacks.

Unwanted castles and forts soon fell into ruin, and their stone was removed for use in other buildings. Some castles became army barracks or military headquarters, while others were converted into homes. Castles did remain in military use in some areas, especially along

Rifles from the Revolutionary War

the land border between Christian central Europe and Muslim Turkish-controlled southeast Europe, while new forts were built in areas of colonial conflict between the European empires, particularly in North America.

Why castles revived

In the A.D. 1800s castles began a new life as living symbols of the medieval world. Many people held a romantic view of that period—those who could not build a complete castle constructed a medieval folly or a classical ruin.

Today castles and forts are vibrant buildings visited by thousands of people each year. They house museums about medieval life and stage reenactments of battles, sieges, and jousts. They are lovingly cared for by stonemasons and conservationists, while archaeologists painstakingly excavate their grounds to discover clues about their history and life. Meanwhile crowds of people wander around the great keep trying to imagine what it must have been like to live inside these great stone walls or face an enemy army camped outside. Castles are now as much a part of our lives as they were when they were first built.

o further . . .

Find out more about the secrets of Fort Sumter: www.civilwarhome.com/ftsumter.htm

d out more about the azing Eureka Stockade: p://users.netconnect.com.au/~ian c/eureka.html

rn more about the Eureka flag: w.ausflag.com.au/flags/eka.html

cover what drove Ludwig II ouild Neuschwanstein Castle: w.german-way.com/ludwig.html

Sound or **lighting engineer**
Helps produce historical reenactments.

Prop and costume maker
Creates historical costumes and artifacts.

Architectural historian
Studies (among other things) 19th-century A.D. castles and follies.

Architect or **designer**
Turns ruined castles into modern homes.

Historian
Advises on the care and restoration of old castles.

Visit McCaig's Folly, a 19th-century Scottish folly imitating the Colosseum in Rome, Italy. www.follies.btinternet.co.uk/argyll.html

Explore Castle Drogo in Devon, England, a 20th-century country house built to look like a castle. Castle Drogo Drewsteignton Near Exeter, England EX6 6PB Phone: 44 1677 433 306 www.nationaltrust.org.uk

Glossary

A.D.
Meaning *anno Domini*—latin for "in the year of our Lord." Christian system of dating events beginning with the year it was believed Christ was born.

archaeology
Study of the past using scientific analysis of material remains, undertaken by archaeologists.

bailey
Courtyard in a castle, also known as a ward.

ballista
Ancient, enormous wheeled crossbow that fired wooden or metal bolts.

barbarian
Primitive or uncivilized person.

barbican
Projecting watchtower (linked to the gatehouse) over the gate of a castle.

barracks
Building used to house soldiers.

bastion
Tower or turret projecting from a wall.

B.C.
Meaning *Before Christ*. Christian system of dating beginning with the birth of Christ—so that when counting years B.C., the lower the number, the later the event.

Bronze Age
Historical period in southern Asian, European, and North African history dating from roughly 3500–1000 B.C., during which people learned to make and use bronze for weapons and tools; it was followed by the Iron Age.

casbah
Arab fortified house or castle.

catapult
Siege machine using a tensed arm that, when released, hurls a rock or other missile at an enemy's castle.

citadel
Fortress built inside a town's walls, often at the highest or most secure point.

concentric castle
Castle with two roughly parallel sets of walls.

Crusades
Series of military campaigns from 1095–1291 launched by Christian Europe to win back control of the Holy Land from its Muslim controllers. Those who went on crusade were known as crusaders.

curtain walls
The walls between the towers of a castle.

donjon
French word for a keep or tower.

drawbridge
Bridge over the moat that could be raised to prevent the enemy from entering the castle.

feudalism
Social system in Western Europe during the Middle Ages in which peasants and other vassals owed allegiance to their feudal lord in return for land and protection.

folly
Modern building in the style of a castle or other ancient monument.

gatehouse
Structure in the outer walls of a castle, usually consisting of two towers on each side of the main entrance.

hill fort
Fortified hilltop surrounded by earth or sto ramparts, often containing a small village.

Holy Land
Land between the Jordan river and the Mediterranean Sea, in what is now Israel a Palestine, where biblical events took place.

Holy Roman Empire
Empire covering modern-day Germany, Switzerland, Austria, northern Italy, and much of the Low Countries that existed from A.D. 962–1806; the emperor owed his allegiance to the pope and was elected from among his fellow rulers.

joust
Combat between two mounted knights.

keep
The stone keep was the center of the castle and the main residence of the owner.

knight
Mounted, heavily armed soldier who served his lord.

Knights Hospitallers
Order of knights first organized in Jerusaler in c. A.D. 1070; their official name was the Knights Hospitallers of St. John of Jerusalem.

ksar
Moroccan fortified village.

magazine
Building storing ammunition and weapons.

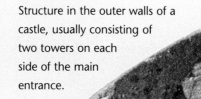

tlet

e mobile wooden shield protecting
ult troops and sappers in a siege.

soleum

e stately tomb housing bodies.

dle Ages

d of European history from the fall of
Roman Empire in the A.D. 400s to the start
e Renaissance during the A.D. 1400s.

t

filled with water, surrounding a castle.

e and bailey

le wooden castle on a mound, with
wbridge connecting it to a bailey.

pon consisting of a long wooden pole,
with a metal spearhead or sharpened end.

im

ious or devout person who makes
rney to a holy place.

e

d of the Roman Catholic Church
me, Italy; his government is known
e papacy. The pope is based at the
an—the papal palace in Rome,
hed to St. Peter's Basilica.

portcullis

Gridlike gate that can be raised and
lowered over the entrance to a castle.

rampart

Earthen embankment surrounding a fort
or castle, often strengthened by stone walls.

sapper

Soldier who digs trenches, tunnels,
and other earthworks.

slingshot

A stone or other missile hurled
out of a sling at an enemy.

Stone Age

Long period of early human history when
stone was the main material for weapons
and tools; it ended after 3500 B.C. at
different times around the world, when
the Bronze Age began.

terra-cotta

Hard, unglazed earthenware made from clay.

tournament

Mock battle designed to test knights.

trebuchet

Pivoting siege machine used
to hurl rocks at an enemy.

Index

Acknowledgments

The publisher would like to thank the following for permission to reproduce their material. Every care has been taken to trace copyright holders. However, if there have been unintentional omissions or failure to trace copyright holders, we apologize and will, if informed, endeavor to make corrections in any future edition.

Key: *b* = bottom, *c* = center, *l* = left, *r* = right, *t* = top

2–3 National Geographic Image Collection (NGIC); 4–5 NGIC; 7 Corbis; 10*t* Art Archive; 10–11 English Heritage; 11*t* English Heritage; 12*bl* Corbis; 12–13 NGIC; 13 Art Archive; 14*l* Corbis; 14–15 Kobal; 15*tl* Mary Evans Picture Library; 15*tr* Zev Radovan; 15*b* Corbis; 16*t* Corbis; 16*b* Corbis; 17*t* Bridgeman Art Library (BAL); 17*bl* Corbis; 17*br* Corbis; 18*t* Corbis; 18–19*t* Corbis; 18–19*b* Corbis; 19*tr* Corbis; 19*c* Corbis; 20 Art Archive; 21 Robert Harding Picture Library; 22*b* Art Archive; 23 Corbis; 23*tr* English Heritage; 24 Alamy; 24–25 DK Images; 25 DK Images; 26*tr* BAL; 27*t* Hutchison Library; 28*tl* Art Archive; 28*cl* HIP/Topham; 28*b* Corbis; 29*t* HIP/Topham; 29*bl* Corbis; 29*br* Skyscan; 30*bl* BAL; 31*tl* BAL; 31 Corbis; 32*br* AKG, London; 33 Corbis; 33*tr* Corbis; 33*bc* BAL; 34*l* Corbis; 34–35 Alamy; 35*tr* Corbis; 36*tl* Corbis; 36*bl* Corbis; 36–37 Corbis; 37*tr* Scala; 37*b* Art Archive; 38*tl* Art Archive; 38*cr* Corbis; 38–39 Getty Images; 39*t* Corbis; 41 Art Archive; 42*tl* Corbis; 42*b* Art Archive; 43*tl* Art Archive; 43*b* Corbis; 45 NGIC; 46*bl* Corbis; 46*br* Corbis; 47*b* Corbis; 48*tl* Corbis; 49*trl* Corbis; 50*bl* Corbis; 50*br* Corbis; 51*bc* Corbis; 51*br* Corbis; 52*cl* Corbis; 52–53 Hulton Getty; 54*c* Art Archive; 54–55 Corbis; 55*tr* Robert Harding Picture Library; 56*b* Corbis; 56–57 NGIC; 57*b* Corbis; 58*b* Corbis; 60–61 NGIC

The publisher would like to thank the following illustrators:
Mark Bristow 64; Robert McKoen and Daniel Shutt 30–31*tl*;
Steve Weston (Linden Artists) 1, 8–9 main artwork, 10–11 main artwork and *tr*, 22–23*tl*, 26–27 main artwork, 30–31 main artwork, 40–41 main artwork, 46–47 main artwork, 48–49 main artwork, 50–51 main artwork, 52–53 main artwork

The author would like to thank Melissa, Peter, and Cee for all their hard work and enthusiasm in editing, designing, and researching this book—and Gill for commissioning it.